TECHNICAL ANALYSIS & MARKET STRUCTURE

The true price action series volume 2

Derby Matoma

CONTENTS

Title Page	
Foreword	1
Market structure	3
Uptrends	8
Downtrends	9
Retracements	10
Now apply the same logic to downtrends.	11
Support and Resistance	12
Resistance	14
Trendlines	15
Uptrend trendlines	16
Downtrends	19
Channeling	22
Final analysis	25
Special acknowledgments	29

FOREWORD

Over the years numerous trading strategies have been developed . Some effective yet some not as effective. Some are straightforward and tidy yet some are shabby.

Some traders use indicators while others don't. Most traders tend to go the indicators way as it requires less thought process. For example EMA cross-overs. All you need to do is check your oscillators and different EMAs if they are crossing and then you execute a trade. The big question is, does that actually work? You tell me. I have no problem with indicators that work, the problem is none seems to work. They don't because they use previous market data trying to predict the future. The market is a weird place one of the rules is "previous market performance is not an indication of future performance", this completely debunks the theory of indicators. Nearly everyone who l has seen success using indicators has a strong underlying strategy that uses indicators for supplementary confirmation.

When l was introduced to trading, the internet quickly prompted me to use crazy stuff like Ichimoku clouds, Bollinger bands, and endless oscillators. This was pretty much unreliable and l paid the price. Later on, l was introduced to price action. I got myself through trendlines, support, and resistance. At this point, l had an understanding of what is market structure. Thereafter l moved to teach myself proper supply and demand, later on, grasped the genius idea behind break and retest.

In this book, l will take you through the market structure, trendlines, and basic support and resistance. Now l can promise you that after finishing this book your understanding of market dynamics and structure will be unmatched. In the end, you should be able to use trendlines to define the market structure and where the market is likely to go. One thing that you have to keep in mind is it's not always about being right while trading but making informed decisions. This will save you from a lot of stupid mistakes in the long run. I am not promising you to beat the market because no one can and noone should. All l want is to give you authentic information and true price action.

As part of my principles,l tend to focus on logic not what everyone says about technical analysis. Everyone's way is the most dangerous.90% of retail traders lose money in securities markets. Hence what the majority says does not matter .

Let's look at what works!

MARKET STRUCTURE

Market structure is the description for market movement of a period of time. They are basically two structures in the market namely **Ranging** and **Trending.**

Ranging Market

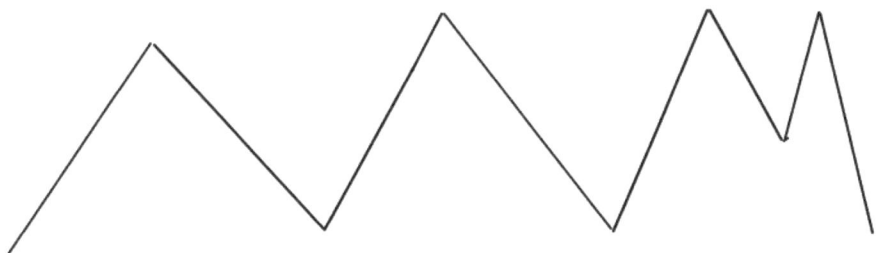

A ranging market is one in which the market is moving up and down resulting in a sideways net movement. Just as shown in the picture above. The markets range because of two reasons

1 Indecision of the market participants - this means there is no consensus as to whether the market should go upward or downwards. Hence sellers and buyers continue to battle producing equal momentum. consequently, the market will be tossed up and down its key levels of interest.

Example

Nb- security can be stocks,bonds ,cyrpto,forex etc

If a security has 100 people repeatedly trying to sell it at $5 and 100 repeatedly people trying to buy it at

$3.50. Given that in-between the price ($3.5 -$5)range people are not interested in security this is what happens :

When the price of the gets to $3.5 the 100 buyers will buy the security. Between $3.50 and $4.99, they won't find anyone to sell to. However when the price to $5.00 the sellers will be waiting for them. (*Remember for sellers to sell they need to buy first*) The sellers will buy from the buyers and sell it at the same price expecting the market to fall. Since there are no buyers till $3.50 the market will move down to $3.50 where there are buyers to buy from the sellers.

So long the market participants are interested in these two market prices $3.50 and $5 the market will continue to range between these two prices. **Contrary to what most people think the market is not moved by the presence of orders it is moved by their absence.** This means at prices where no one is doing anything the market just cruises through. For the same reason, the market will only stop at the far ends where there are orders to be executed and because no one is active in-between, the market just passes through without facing resistance.

2.The other reason the market can be ranging is because of supply and demand. This is almost the same as in example 1, however, supply and demand explain various situations especially the ones the market leaves a price level without getting all the orders filled .

Let's say there is high demand for a cryptocurrency at

$4 and there is an enormous supply for the cryptocurrency at $7.Both the supply and the demand at these levels are unquenchable. This is what's going to happen:

When the market gets to $4 it will shoot upside because there are too many people buying at this level, however, most people won't get their orders executed at $4 because the prices moved too fast that they could not get in the market in time or their pending orders were not triggered in. So these folks will be waiting for the market to come back to $4 dollars again *(note that these are not retail traders as most retail traders have no particular price levels of interest banks do though)*. The market will soar to $7 and the supply will trigger in quickly selling the crypto down. The same situation happens to suppliers not all of them get their orders triggered so they wait for the market to come back up again to $7 for them to sell at a high price. If the price returns to $7 it will drop down to $4 and the cycle repeats until the supply and demand gets exhausted in both ends exhaust.

Both scenarios will leave the market bouncing up and down. In my own economic terms, there is an "equilibrium range" in a ranging market. This is because sellers and buyers are agreeing not at a particular price but a range of prices hence the market will move up and down within this range.

Here is the catch of the story the most markets are ranging 70% of the time. Now, this is a big deal because it means 70% of the time the market is not going anyway it's just moving up and down. Sadly retail traders trade 110% of the time not knowing the market is not going anyway.

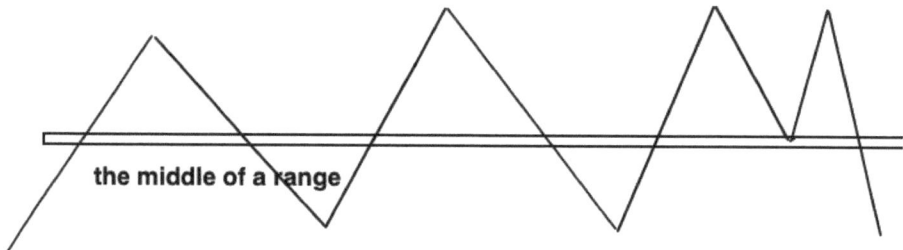

The worst part of ranges is that most retail traders execute their trades at the middle points of the range. Can you imagine how much they suffer at both buying and selling scenarios as markets move in their direction for a while before firing back to wipe out their suffering accounts? This is usually due to lagging indicators. Think of it in a range your moving average indicator will show you that the market is now moving upwards when the market had *already started moving upwards three* hours ago. This implies you are going to execute your trade at the middle of a range or at the upper end of a range. You will be executing orders in the middle range shown in the picture. The market will go your way and reverse only to hit your stop loss before moving in your direction again. Imagine the frustration!
I don't blame anyone who gets played by the market in a range because it's very hard to know when the market has started to range. I have attached a real-life example

of a ranging market from Nas 100

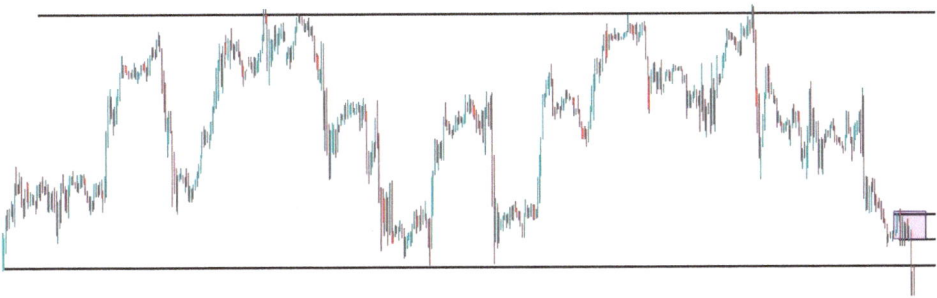

In typical live markets, a range looks like the above picture with defined points of moving and moving down

Trending Markets

The trending market is everyone's favorite. You have probably had people say the trend is your friend. However, be advised that your trend only comes 30% of the time. You should then do away with trying to trade 110 % of the time if you want to ride trends. The market can trend in two directions upside or downside.

Trending markets have two forms (a) uptrends
(b) downtrends

UPTRENDS

An uptrend is a movement characterized by the market moving to the upside. It is important to note that the market does not shoot up without drawbacks. The market forms higher highs and higher lows successfully.

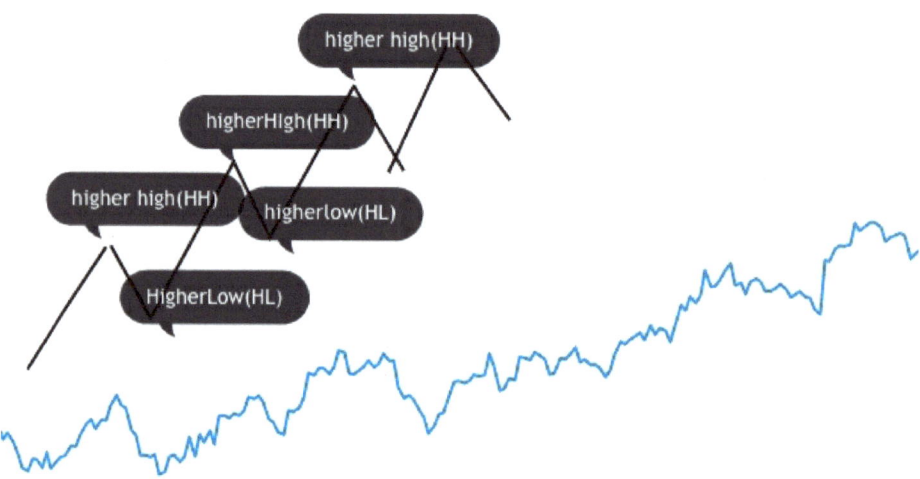

In the above scenario, the market is reaching a new high for every movent.The high is usually higher than the previous one.The high is also known as the swing point.The market also experiences retracements hence comes higher lows or swing lows.The succeeding swing low is higher than the previous swing low. Clearly, the rule has a few exemptions as shown in the real

market data in blue, since in some instances the swing low would be lower than the previous swing low. The implication of this movement is buyers are in control and you probably want to be going long as the trend may continue for many long periods. It is in these moments that the market moves in defined directions.

DOWNTRENDS

Downtrends are when the market moves down. Note that the markets don't just plunge down without retracing.

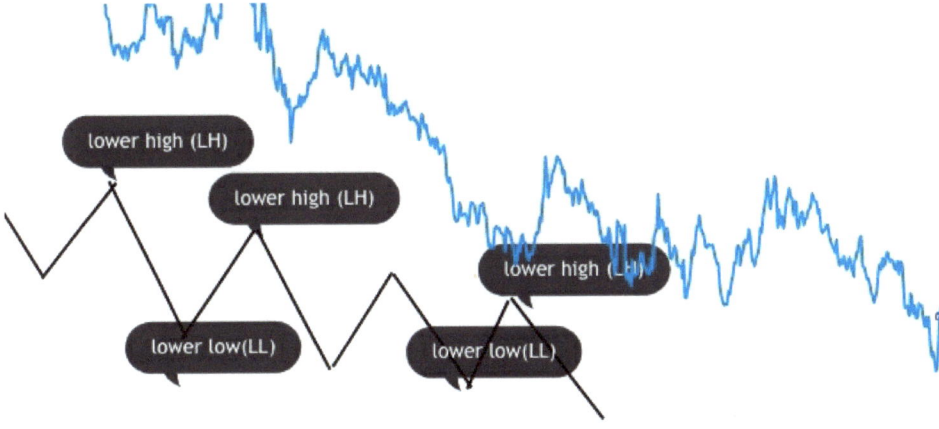

The market moves in a series of lower lows and lower highs. The previous highs are not surpassed neither are the previous lows. This implies sellers are in control and are pushing the market lower every time they get a chance.

RETRACEMENTS

There many names for retracements some call them swing high/swing low, corrections, pullbacks, etc. I have heard of someone saying think of it as if the market breathes, so as it moves it takes short breaks to breath. Whichever way you want to understand it make sure you know the proper logic behind the movement. Let's say in a bullish market, the market is clearly rallying. The bulls are in control continuously buying. Now at some point, some traders will decide to take profits. As a rule of thumb to close a buy order the trader executes a sell order, this is a must and the market can not function without this principle. If you buy security to sell it you have to short it. Through shorting they create a small supply hence the markets will experience a drawback as they are individuals selling. However, take note that these individuals are not the rest of the pack. The big picture remains intact, the market movers will be pretty much long. Hence even with these small retracements, the market will continue going long.

NOW APPLY THE SAME LOGIC TO DOWNTRENDS.

In downtrends, pullbacks are a result of sellers taking their profits, this in turn gives an impression of short-term buy orders. As a result, the market will experience a short-lived uptrend.

SUPPORT AND RESISTANCE

Support is a lower price level that is continuously being yet pushing the market afloat or up. Think of it as a basketball. The basketball is shoved down yet the floor makes sure the ball bounces up. That's how support works, it keeps the market bounces up.

The purple rectangle shows where the market was finding its support. The support is important in determining the market as it shows where buyers are most active. **I know you are expecting me to tell you to buy at support but NO, I am not.** Never at any point have I encouraged anyone to buy at support. Your duty is to recognize where support is so as to have a glimpse of what is happening in the market. The reason why I don't encourage anybody to trade at support is that you can't tell when the level is going to break. It's funny that people say the longer the market bounces up off a level the longer the level will sustain. Nothing can be further from the truth. The more it bounces off a level the weaker it becomes here is why. The demand will get exhausted most people interested in that price will get their orders executed eventually and abandon the level. If no one is interested in buying at that particular level the market will just cruise through *its way better to trade the break & retest of support, not the support itself* (this is an advanced topic not to be covered in this book).For the sake of understanding the market structure **just mark** support.

RESISTANCE

If you managed to understand support as the floor then you can as well consider resistance as the roof. This the price level at which the market continuously falls from. Similarly do not try trade of this level as it is unreliable.

As shown in the picture the market repeatedly fails to break the level hence as a result of its resistance to being broken we call it resistance level. It's important to note that this level is a key price of interest as there is much supply interested around this price. Nb, *it is smart to mark support and resistance as zones not as definite prices using a line.*

TRENDLINES

Also known as dynamic support and resistance trendlines are used to show the prevalent market direction or trend. This is done by joining 2 or 3 immediate swing points in any market. After joining the two points the trendline can be extrapolated to show the expected direction of the market.

Trendlines can be used to map out chart patterns like triangles, flags, and wedges.In general, they bring out the market structure. We will not cover chart patterns in this book however the basis of chart patterns is joining to swing points just like in trendlines.

One common problem traders have is they can be very subjective when drawing trendlines. This is very detrimental when one needs to know the market movement. This is caused by traders trying to force their imagination into existence. This results in traders forcing the market to follow their own trendlines not their trendlines following the market. There is need to draw trendlines in an unbiased manner with a focus put on the two most recent swing lows or swing highs.

Since the market trends two ways, there are two forms of trendlines,uptrend trendlines and downtrend trendlines.

UPTREND TRENDLINES

In uptrends, we join the most recent two swing lows.

Using picture below

Note that my trendline only focused on the first 2 swings and 1 did not try to force the line to fit the third swing too. In most cases, the third swing will effortlessly fit in the trendline. With a trendline in place, the market direcion is not hard to determine.

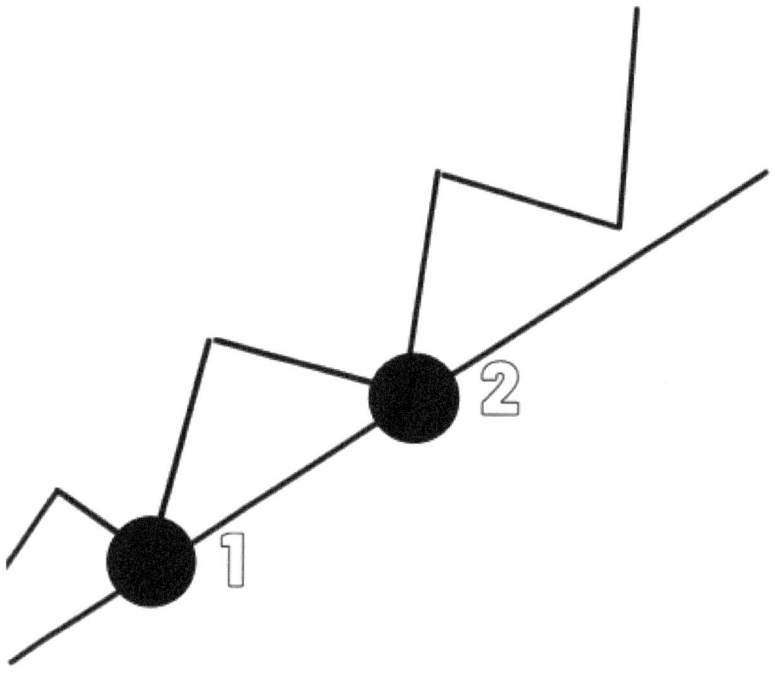

More so we can also try to figure out where the pullbacks might reach before continuing with trade. The picture is a mere textbook example we will soon delve into real market examples.

In the real market example below, emphasis is put on the most immediate two sing lows. An important point to note is that the two swing lows l chose are very significant. It is clear that the two swings resulted in very high swing highs which makes them key. They are plenty of swing lows in the trend however they did not push much to contribute to the uptrend.

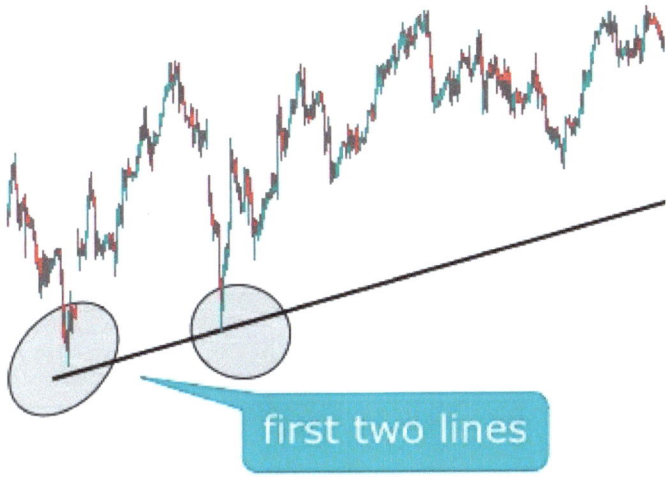

Every swing connected produced a high, higher than the previous high in the market.

One common mistake traders make is trying to find a line of best fit. This is helpful in traditional statistics and data presentation but it's not the case in financial markets. You don't have to spend time looking for a line that gathers the most amount of swing highs and swing lows. We focus on the relevant swings only.
The relevant swings lows have the following characteristics :
   1. Most recent
   2. Produces significant highs in an uptrend.

DOWNTRENDS

Downtrends operate with the same principle as uptrends. In downtrends, *we focus on swing highs which push to produce lower lows.* As a rule of thumb, the most immediate significant two swings highs are more important than the old ones.

The trendline connects the first two swing highs without trying to fit the third swing high. From the picture below, it is very clear that the trend is down and most swing highs are coming below or hitting the down trendline. There are a few exceptions to the rules since outliers are every where. You can expect some swing highs to surpass the trendline however in most cases the candlesticks which result in these high usually close below the trendline.

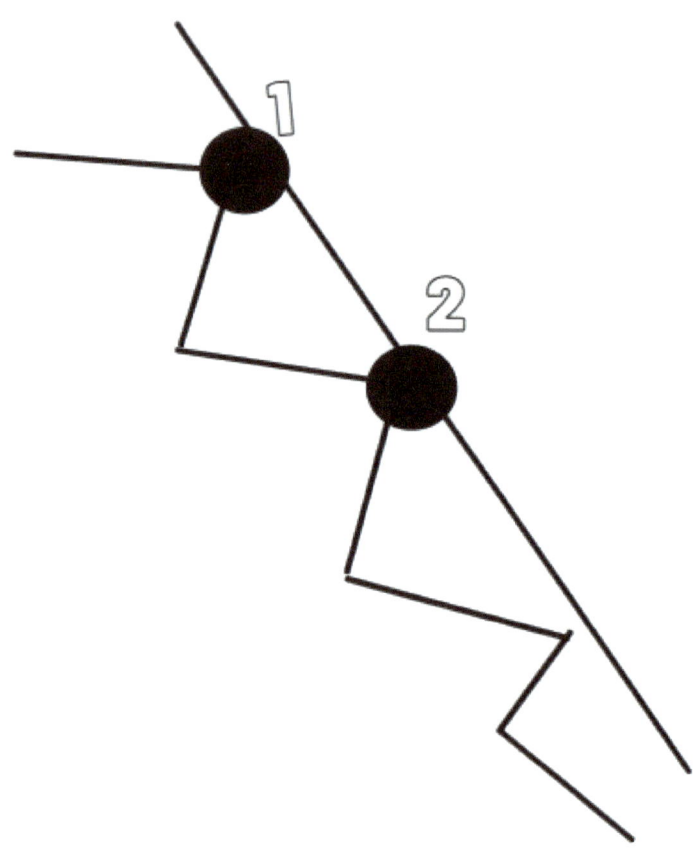

The above shows a downtrend. You must be wondering why the first high was not joined. This is because the succeeding high is at the same price and it produced quite a lower swing low than the previous one. Remember factors that make a swing relevant. This, therefore, puts the third swing the most immediate swing which the market respected.

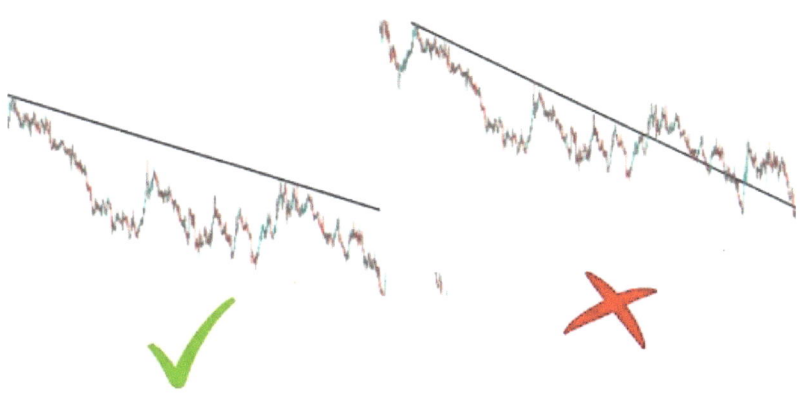

Always remember to filter off the noise and focus on the relevant swings to deduce market structure.

CHANNELING

If you have studied most price action charts you will realize their trendlines are put out in the form of channels. This is not hard to do at all. To do this you just have to add another line on the other side of your trendline, this is not very relevant however it helps in producing a clear picture of the market structure.

Here is what typical channels look like

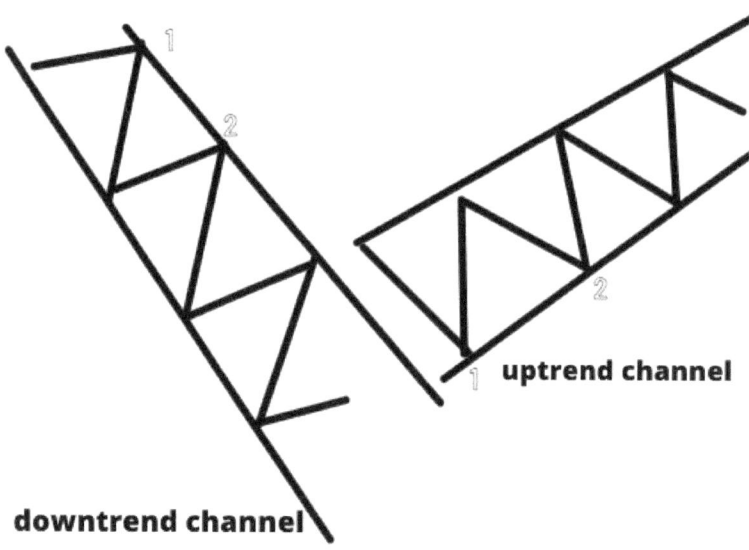

There aren't any strict rules as to how to map out the channel. The main focus should be put on bringing out a non-subjective trendline. Eventually, you should realize drawing channels is not different from drawing chart patterns.

Examples

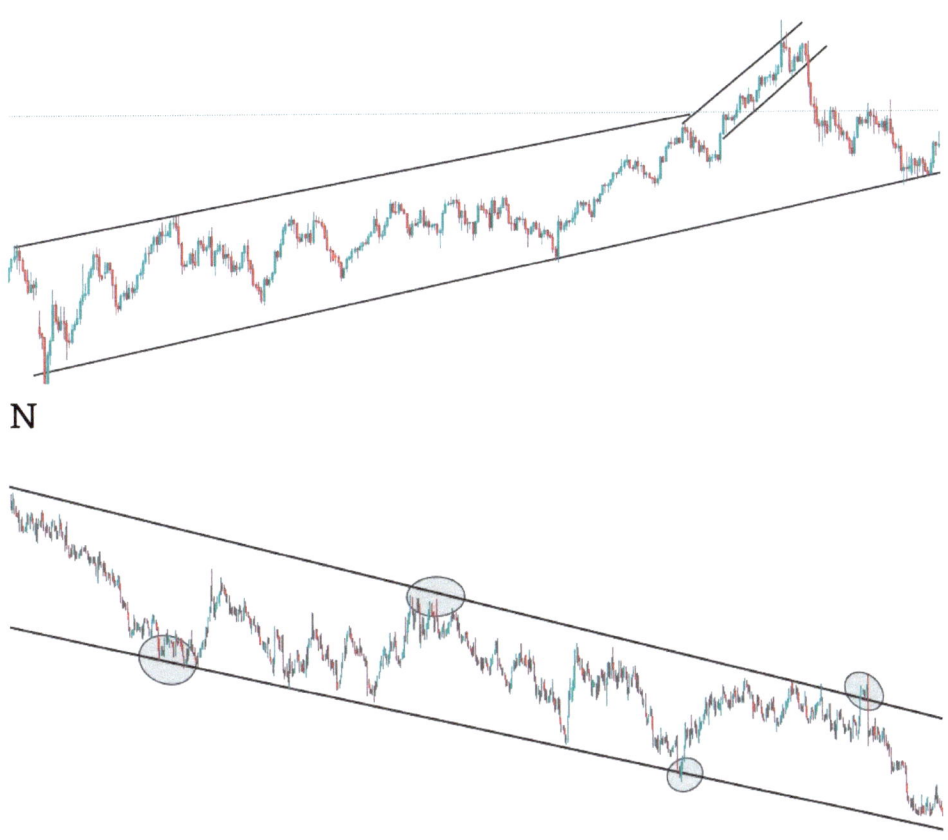

Looking at these examples .Try channelling trends from your charts.Focus and see if you can say something about the market using the channel .In most cases after putting channels you filter off noise and focus on the most important data .Focusing in relevant market information is the sole reason one should put channels on trends.

FINAL ANALYSIS

Using the information given in this book you should be able to say something about the market structure and possible directions. I will share with you random charts and l want you to explain to anyone how the market is moving. Focus on explaining the movement in terms of buyers and sellers. Note that in my charts l will use both support & resistance as well as trendlines to make sure we have a clear picture of the market's activities.

Examples
1

2

DERBY TENDAI MATOMA

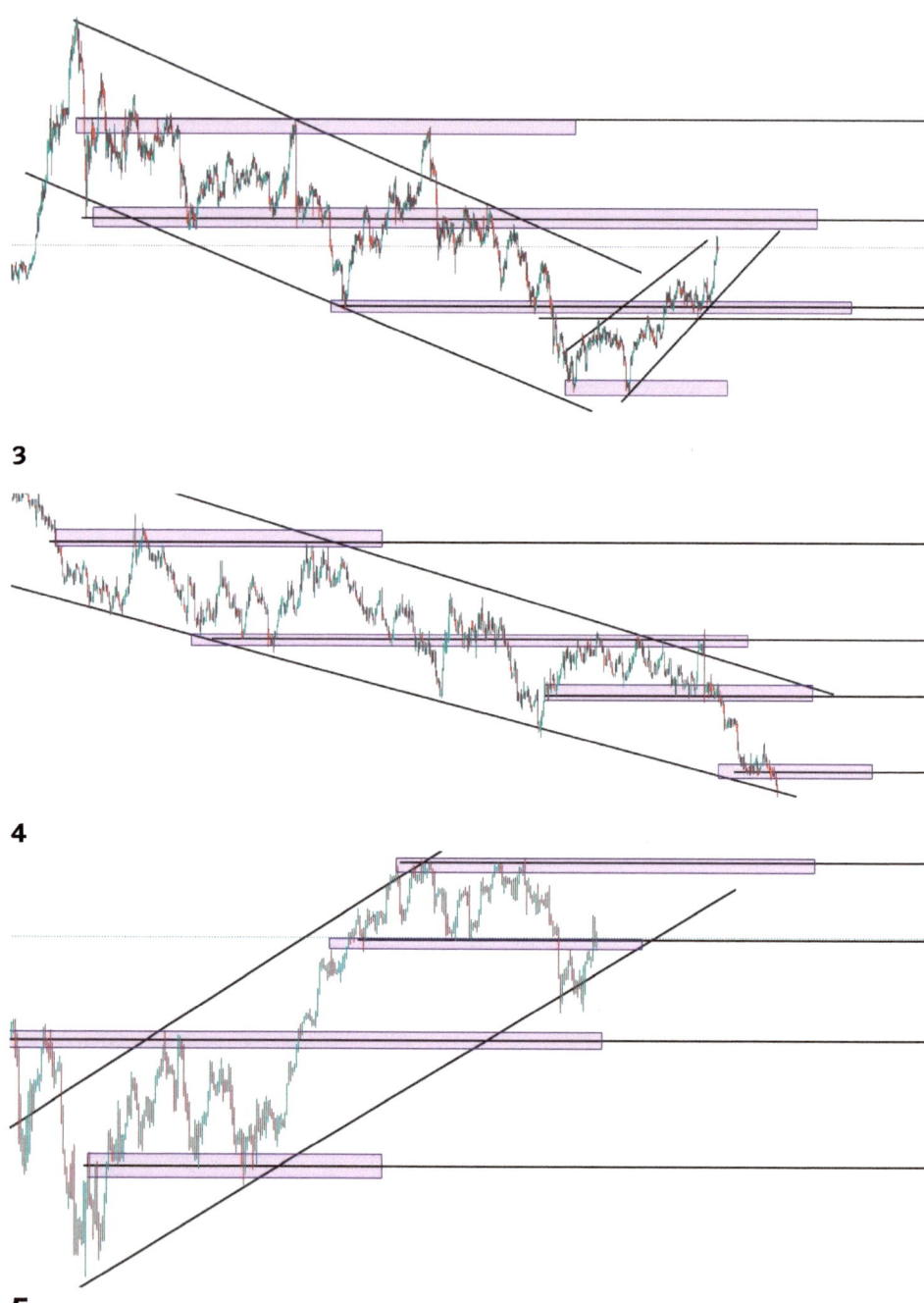

3

4

5

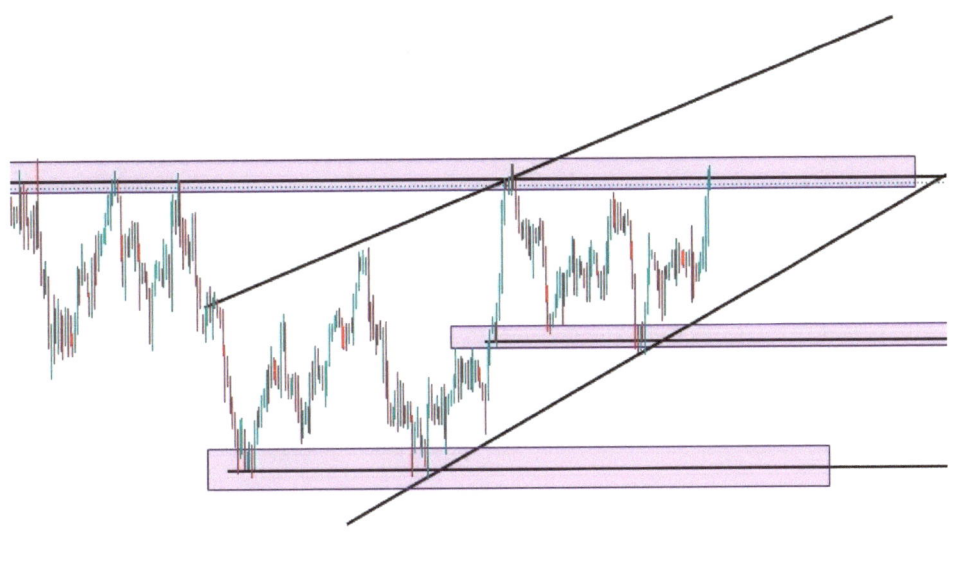

If you can analyze your chart as shown above you have separated yourself from the rest of the pack. Congratulations !!

This book focused on analyzing market structure and understanding market movement. The focus was to impute a general understanding of how the market moves and develop a strategy premised on that.

I have to say this is a doorway to building trading strategies in various markets. In the entire book 1 never mentioned opening trades, not to say the information given is irrelevant. If you research more and practice you might get a serious edge using this little information. However, knowing market structure only is not enough to open trades

There are two more books to go in this series, these will focus on trading break and retest & supply and demand. The approach will unveil will surely blow your mind that 1 can promise. We focus on how and where banks and huge institutions execute their orders.

In the following Ebooks, I will give out the comprehensive strategy with all the essential blocks assembled. You can also check out my Udemy course that way you will easily get the other set of Ebooks

Always remember success is a journey and you can not skip steps. Take it one step at a time.

SPECIAL ACKNOWLEDGMENTS

I want to thank me for dedicating time to my writeups. I also want to thank my family for supporting my work. Most importantly I want to thank you the **reader**, you are the reason why this book exists.

www.ingramcontent.com/pod-product-compliance
Lightning Source LLC
Chambersburg PA
CBHW040300220526
45473CB00002B/539

Note from the Author

So many renters want to invest in Real Estate but they're not sure how the process works. As a Real Estate Professional, it is my responsibility to help educate you on the home buying experience, so you can have a successful closing on your first property. This book will walk you through the steps that you can expect on this journey. Let me show you how to gain generational wealth for your family's future.